# Unlocking the Quantum Kingdom

Explore the Intersection
of Faith and Quantum Science to Realize
Your Spiritual Potential and Life Purpose!

by

Dr. Robert Rodich

# Unlocking the Quantum Kingdom

Explore the Intersection
of Faith and Quantum Science to Realize
Your Spiritual Potential and Life Purpose!

by

Dr. Robert Rodich DD., Ph.D.

9436 Impala Drive
Foley, Alabama 36535
USA

Docrodich.com

Unlocking the Quantum Kingdom

*Explore the Intersection of Faith and Quantum Science to Realize Your Spiritual Potential and Life Purpose!*

Copyright © 2024 Dr. Robert Rodich

The views and content expressed in this book are those of the author and may not necessarily reflect the views and doctrine of Dr. Ron Horner or of LifeSpring International Ministries, Inc.

Scripture is taken from the New King James Version®. Copyright © 1982 by Thomas Nelson. Used by permission. All rights reserved. (Unless otherwise noted.)

Scripture quotations are taken from the Amplified® Bible (AMP), Copyright © 1954, 1958, 1962, 1964, 1965, 1987 by The Lockman Foundation.

Scripture quotations marked (KJV) are taken from the King James Version, public domain.

All rights reserved. This book is protected by the copyright laws of the United States of America. This book may not be copied or reprinted for commercial gain or profit. The use of short quotations or occasional page copying for personal or group study is permitted and encouraged. Permission will be granted upon request.

Any trademarks mentioned or used are the property of their respective owners.

Additional copies available at docrodich.com

ISBN 13 TP: 978-1-962808-11-8

ISBN 13 eBook: 978-1-962808-12-5

Cover Design by Darian Horner Design (www.darianhorner.com)

Images: 123rf.com #181866926

First Edition: November 2024

10 9 8 7 6 5 4 3 2 1

Printed in the United States of America

# Table of Contents

Dedication .................................................................... 1

Acknowledgments......................................................... 3

Recommendations ........................................................ 5

Introduction ................................................................. 9

Chapter 1 Quantum in Our Daily Lives............................ 13

Chapter 2 What Adam Lost ............................................ 17

Chapter 3 The Basics of Quantum .................................. 25

Chapter 4 The Wonders of Scalar Energy ....................... 31

Chapter 5 Momentum ................................................... 37

Chapter 6 The Way, the Truth, and the Life .................... 45

Chapter 7 Only for the Bold ........................................... 51

Chapter 8 Quantum Has a Designed Mechanical Side ....... 59

Chapter 9 Expanded Thinking......................................... 65

Chapter 10 Let's Plug in Some Examples............................ 75

Chapter 11 The Song of Our Realms................................. 83

Chapter 12 Conclusion..................................................... 89

Appendix A .................................................................... 93

The Relationship Between God's Breath,
Light, Fire, & Glory in Creation .......................................... 93

Appendix B ................................................................... 101

How Gemstones Can Help Our Walk .............................. 101

Appendix C ................................................................... 107

Flavia Diaz's Encounters ................................................ 107

Appendix D ................................................................... 123

Medallions .................................................................... 123

Description ................................................................... 131

About the Author .......................................................... 133

# Dedication

I want to dedicate this book to my dad, Stan Rodich. He was indeed my hero. He always had my back in life and prayer, and I am sure he still does now that he is in Heaven. We were fortunate to have him with us for eighty-nine years and eight months, and he displayed remarkable strength until the end.

While reviewing his papers after his passing, I discovered several writings on quantum principles. Given his engineering background, he clearly explored concepts that aligned closely with the themes presented in this book. I am honored to complete this work in his memory. I'm finishing this for you. Pops!

*My dad at the Ark Experience in Kentucky, 2016, holding the door to the ark—how fitting!*

## Acknowledgments

Few things in life are worth doing alone, and this journey has been no exception. My deepest gratitude goes to my wife, Laura, who is always there with a helping hand and a listening ear. She is truly one hundred percent on this journey with me.

My friend and brother Bryant Jackson, your constant encouragement and inspiration mean more than words can express.

I am also thankful for Dr. Ron Horner, whose leadership brings both stability and confidence to everyone within his sphere of influence.

And a special thanks to Flavia Diaz, who exemplifies all that engaging Heaven can bring to a person's life, inspiring us all to embrace Heaven as our true reality.

## Recommendations

It is an absolute honor to recommend *Unlocking the Quantum Kingdom*, a profound work by my dear friend Dr. Robert Rodich, whom we all lovingly call Doc. This book is the culmination of his deep spiritual wisdom, drawn from years of experience walking intimately with God and exploring the mysteries of the spirit. Doc has an incredible gift for making even the most complex spiritual truths accessible, inviting readers to lean in, reflect deeply, and grow in their understanding of who they are in Christ.

At the heart of this book is Doc's unwavering passion for revealing identity. He shows readers that we are not mere spectators in life but governing sons on the Earth, called to live in the fullness of our divine purpose. His teaching is both fearless and enlightening, venturing into the realm of quantum—an area that can often feel overwhelming—but with his careful guidance, it becomes clear, practical, and life-giving.

What makes *Unlocking the Quantum Kingdom* even more powerful is how it highlights that as we embrace this understanding, we, as sons, will begin to entangle more and more with the Father in Heaven. In this divine connection, we will live, move, and have our being aligning with His heartbeat and purpose for us. Doc paints a beautiful picture of what it means to walk in oneness with God, allowing the flow of Heaven to permeate every part of our existence.

*Stephanie Stanfill*
Executive Assistant
LifeSpring Int'l Ministries

..........

In the few years I've known Doc, we have both been amazed at all Heaven has to show us. No matter how much we learn, we feel like we have barely scratched the surface of unpacking the revelation that Heaven has for us.

When I first saw the material he had a year and a half ago, I knew it needed to be put in book form. We did so for his first book, *Moving Toward Sonship*.

I did not have to coax him to put this new and explosive revelatory information into book form. He was already doing it. It has been an honor and privilege to work with Doc, as we both simply want to see the sons mature as the Father desire. You will enjoy this book. You may have to pause, ponder, and re-read some segments because of the richness of the revelation, but you will be challenged and changed, nonetheless.

Blessings as you read and digest this Porter House Steak with all the trimmings.

*Dr. Ron M. Horner*
Founder
LifeSpring Int'l Ministries

# Introduction

I would like to clarify that I am not a quantum physicist. My background lies in ministry and what many refer to as alternative medicine, in which I hold doctorates in both fields. My focus on energy and frequency enables me to test and understand concepts that may elude others. God has instilled in me a scientific curiosity that drives my research into the "how" and "why" of various phenomena.

Recently, I purchased a scalar energy health device that uses quantum scalar energy waves. This experience has deepened my interest in quantum theory and its connections to Creation and God's Kingdom. Because I have been familiar with many aspects of how the quantum kingdom operates, I have been able to ask God how things work. As a result, I have received guidance from Him on these matters.

This book represents my effort to share these insights, illustrating our preciousness to Him and the wonders He desires to perform through us all.

We find ourselves at a pivotal moment in our journey on Earth. Our purpose and assignment is to be restored to the heart of God and then visibly demonstrate His Kingdom on Earth. We have the advantage of reviewing the successes and failures of our brethren for the last six thousand years.

History reveals numerous movements of God, each offering valuable lessons. Through my study of these outpourings, one striking observation emerges: the absence of the full demonstration of the "greater things than these" that the Lord Jesus mentioned in John 14:12. While we could all speculate as to why such demonstration has only been sporadic to this point in history, I can say that perhaps the answer lies in the fact that we may need to expand our thinking to uncover the reasons behind this phenomenon.

> *I assure you and most solemnly say to you, anyone who believes in Me [as Savior] will also do the things that I do; and he will do even greater things than these [in extent and outreach] because I am going to the Father. (John 14:12, AMP)*

Expanding our thinking does not mean we throw out the foundational truths of our faith. I suggest that the absolute truth of God's Word contains everything we need to succeed in our earthly mission. Simply put, "expanded thinking" begins with cultivating a deeper intimacy in our personal relationship with God. This means loving on Him and, hanging out with Him, and even entering more fully into His heart. It is within this intimacy that our eyes are opened to the depths of what was really accomplished on the cross and how that translates to us personally.

We must be bold enough to embrace the full meaning of Scripture as applicable to all of us today rather than deferring its fullness to a distant future, as many tend to do. This understanding includes the many spiritual technologies that are hinted at in Scripture. We need to be aware that some of these "truths" have already been co-opted and are being used by those who operate in darkness, albeit in limited ways.

God's Kingdom is here and now and is available to all who would press in.

The answers we seek have always been around us, yet our understanding and vision have been purposely dumbed down (veiled), preventing God's children from discovering His true magnificence and His genuine plan for us. We are here on assignment, yet most of us either partially or never fulfill that assignment because we are burdened with teaching that is off point or we have not fully risen above the ramifications of the fall.

In recent years a new field of science known as quantum physics has captured significant attention. As scientists have delved deeper into this arena, they have begun to uncover operational principles that challenge and reshape the understanding of our reality. These scientists tell us that quantum mechanics function like an "energetic grid" that operates outside the confines of time and space and has characteristics that are quite different than those we normally experience in everyday life.

In this book, I hope to present the operating principles of quantum physics in a way that is complementary to our faith, guiding us toward a deeper understanding. My hope is that we may reach a point where we can respond to the groanings of creation, awaiting its restoration to fullness.

# Chapter 1
# Quantum in Our Daily Lives

In 1900, Max Planck became the first to introduce the concept of quantum physics. While classical physics explains matter and energy based on what we see, quantum physics delves into the unseen forces at play, describing what goes on behind the scenes at the smallest, most fundamental levels. Quantum also allows a person, object, or energy to exist in multiple places simultaneously. The scientific community has wrestled with these revolutionary ideas. Even Einstein referred to these quantum realities as "spooky" because of their seemingly supernatural nature.

As believers, we absolutely know Who and what this unseen source is. The question I am asking is if science is now merely catching up to the established order of creation, rebranding it under different terminology. Because many scientists are heavily invested in the theory of evolution, they may struggle to acknowledge that the complexities of the universe are the result of a Creator's design. Admitting this would mean recognizing that the Creator's work is far more creative, intelligent, and powerful than anything that could arise from a single cell or a mere spark. It would also require them to answer to a higher power instead of adhering solely to their god of science.

Perhaps scientists are not the only ones failing to give credit where it is due. The church, too, has often fallen into a similar bias, confining God within a religious box.

Within our ranks are those who acknowledge the supernatural and those who do not. Those who lack this recognition often adopt a more legalistic mindset, placing greater emphasis on good works, church attendance, and evangelism. While these practices are certainly important, they represent only a portion of the broader demonstration of the Kingdom.

Among those who acknowledge the miraculous, there seems to be a prevalent bias that the majority of supernatural acts that do happen are attributed to the "sovereignty of God" or the "special giftings" of the Holy Spirit, which, of course, those on the receiving end are ever grateful. Again, there is more to the full demonstration of the Kingdom.

While both camps agree people need a new birth to enter the Kingdom, I long for the day when we agree that the demonstration of this living Kingdom would be hard for the unsaved to deny when they see us manifest the "greater things" Jesus talked about. Let us explore how this could be possible.

We already have the "Word," God's sovereign acts, and the gifts of the Holy Spirit—is it possible that there is yet another platform to demonstrate the Kingdom in a way to fulfill "on Earth as it is in Heaven?"

> *And he said unto them, "When ye pray, say, 'Our Father which art in Heaven, Hallowed be thy name. Thy kingdom come. Thy will be done, as in Heaven, so in Earth.'" (Luke 11:2, KJV)*

Is there a platform that might explain the mechanisms Jesus tapped into when He turned water into wine, raised the dead, walked on water, or walked through a wall after His resurrection? We need to broaden our perspective to recognize that such a platform exists: it lies in the operational principles of the quantum grid and its energy flow of scalar energy. By understanding these concepts, we can gain insight into the science behind the supernatural and understand how we might operate in it as well.

# Chapter 2
# What Adam Lost

In a sense, the quantum understanding of reality reveals that waveforms operate like an interactive grid that holds the potential for observable reality. These waveforms remain neither solid nor fixed until they interact with something or are observed. This reality only responds to God himself and mankind at the highest level. This unseen grid is engaged through *frequency* and *intention*.

> *As a man thinketh in his heart, so is he. (Proverbs 23:7, KJV)*

Humanity's ability to interact with this quantum grid and shape our reality is fundamental to the image of God within us. Let us now take a deeper look at what Adam lost and passed down to the rest of humanity.

The Bible serves as our "need to know" resource, establishing God's sovereignty while documenting the successes and failures of His children throughout history. It also provides the foundational guide for equipping us to fulfill our assignment (destiny).

Let me interject that there has been much conversation lately about the Bible being incomplete or dumbed down. My take is that there could well be a deeper understanding that does not translate its full meaning into English; however, this does not affect the foundational truths of the Bible. Nor should we look to gnostic or mystical writings or personal experiences to fill in the blanks. We have the greatest teacher of all time in the Holy Spirit, who can fill in those blanks. Engagements and experiences should only make the truth of the Bible more real, making it more alive while adding greater insights and never replacing its truth with a "greater" revelation.

Our purpose, once we are restored to God (John 3:3-7), is to begin cleaning up the generational and positional messes inside of us that we were born into or that we came into agreement with (see my book, *Moving Toward Sonship*).[1] It is as we deal with our inner issues that we gain many of the skills required to move on to our full assignment: restoring creation (Genesis 2:15). And restoring creation is more than having bigger tomatoes or strawberries in our garden.

John 3:3-7:

*Jesus answered him, "I assure you and most solemnly say to you, unless a person is born again [reborn from above—spiritually transformed, renewed, sanctified], he cannot [ever] see and experience the Kingdom of God."*

*⁴ Nicodemus said to Him, "How can a man be born when he is old? He cannot enter his mother's womb a second time and be born, can he?" ⁵ Jesus answered, "I assure you and most solemnly say to you, unless one is born of water and the Spirit, he cannot [ever] enter the Kingdom of God. [Ezek 36:25-27] ⁶ That which is born of the flesh is flesh [the physical is merely physical], and that which is born of the Spirit is spirit.*

---

[1] Dr. Robert Rodich, *Moving Toward Sonship*. (LifeSpring Publishing, 2023).

*⁷ Do not be surprised that I have told you, 'You must be born again [reborn from above—spiritually transformed, renewed, sanctified].'" (AMP)*

Genesis 2:15:

*And the LORD God took the man, and put him into the garden of Eden to dress it and to keep it. (KJV)*

Mankind has five aspects to their divine assignment:

1. **Protection** – Caring for creation and humanity (Genesis 2:15).
2. **Provision** – Providing for family (1 Timothy 5:8).
3. **Proclamation** – Speaking up against injustice (Jeremiah 22:3).
4. **Presentation** – Husbands caring for their wives as Christ cares for the Church (Ephesians 5:25-27).
5. **Praise** – Offering continual praise to God (Hebrews 13:15), completing the love cycle that begins and ends with the Father.

In these five areas, we find the inspiration to influence and change the world through quantum interaction. More on that later. Remember that God rules the cosmos, and we are assigned to Earth.

As the Father leads us to influence reality on Earth—whether by bringing a soul into the Kingdom or transforming the course of a nation, it is key to know how to tap into the Father's heart. It is the Father's emotions for a situation that supercharges our words with quantum power and His unique design. This is how we begin to change the world!

Consider this: We begin in the heart of the Father, who knew us before we were placed in our mother's womb (Jeremiah 1:5). If the goal were to return to Him after salvation, what would be the purpose of our existence here? Instead, our lives are part of a much larger plan to restore all creation to its complete design, which was altered due to a great cosmic rebellion (Luke 10:17-20).

> *Before I formed thee in the belly I knew thee; and before thou camest forth out of the womb I sanctified thee, and I ordained thee a prophet unto the nations. (Jeremiah 1:5, KJV)*

> *[17] The seventy returned with joy, saying, "Lord, even the demons are subject to us in Your name." [18] He said to them, "I watched Satan fall from Heaven like [a flash of] lightning.*
> *[19] Listen carefully: I have given you authority [that you now possess] to tread on serpents and scorpions, and [the ability to exercise authority] over all the power of*

> *the enemy (Satan); and nothing will [in any way] harm you.*
> *²⁰ Nevertheless do not rejoice at this, that the spirits are subject to you, but rejoice that your names are recorded in Heaven." (Luke 10:17-20, AMP)*

We can glimpse our new blueprint by looking at Adam's abilities before his fall from grace and a glimpse of even greater possibilities by looking at what our Savior demonstrated here on Earth as the Son of Man.

Adam was a being of light. He walked with his spirit forward. He likely had multidimensional abilities. Certainly, his intellect was not limited. He was also able to meet with God daily and in person. Think about that!

Then, consider all that Jesus taught and accomplished (John 21:25). His character, love, integrity, holiness, miracles, and teachings all point to the possibilities we can share, which points to the importance of quantum. This is where understanding quantum entanglement is so vital.

> *And there are also many other things which Jesus did, the which, if they should be written everyone, I suppose that even the world itself could not contain the books that should be written. Amen. (John 21:25, KJV)*

John 14:20 is a picture of quantum entanglement with the Godhead.

*I am in My Father, and you in Me, and I in you.*

If we grasp this truth and do not let our cognitive dissonance get in the way, we will never be the same! By definition, quantum entanglement means that the same influence present in one part exists in all parts at the very exact moment and with the same influence. Yes, filters and static can get in the way; however, this is our present reality, and all we need to do is get out of the way and learn to operate in what is already a part of our "born again" nature.

> ***Shortcut alert:*** *Learn that you can step directly into Father's heart. There, His love defines you, grounds you, brings balance to you and your realms, and melts away trauma and frustration. This is effective because nearly all distractions cannot stand in His love.*

Practice this daily! Let us build our understanding to make this our reality.

# Chapter 3
# The Basics of Quantum

I need to share a point of understanding before I explain quantum. Modern science generally operates under the belief that we live in an electromagnetic universe. This is a misconception—we live in a *magneto-electric universe*. **These are not the same.**

In Genesis 1:3-25, the Bible says, *"God said, Let there be light."* This phrase underscores a vital idea: *magneto-electric* starts first with a sound. When God spoke, the sound (resonance, frequency) came first, which then generated a magneto-electric field. This field subsequently created electromagnetic fields, from which light emerged.

The key takeaway is that when God commanded light to exist, a series of events was set into motion. The starting point was sound, which means that electromagnetism—what science typically focuses on—comes later in the process. By emphasizing electromagnetism, mainstream science is overlooking the true source: sound and the magneto-electric fields it generates. Sound, not electromagnetism, is the origin from which everything unfolds, but modern science often begins its exploration with what is already visible rather than seeking the underlying cause.

If you do not understand this idea, then everything I explain moving forward will be impossible to grasp. The reason is that quantum processes are activated through sound—specifically through voice and frequency—to which the quantum grid responds. As we will discuss, quantum is God's delivery system by which the saints will participate in the process of creating a greater Heaven-based footprint on the Earth.

One could say that the quantum grid exists because God exists; it is a part of Him, holding all things together by His word. In these final days, God is revealing this "family secret" to us so that we can carry out our mission more effectively.

## The Definition of Quantum

Quantum physics is the study of matter and energy at the most basic level, focusing on how the smallest parts of creation behave. Before quantum physics, science focused on the components of the atom. While it is very interesting that the components of an atom resemble a solar system, physical science neglects the field that holds it all together. Quantum physics seeks to explain these unseen forces that operate at the tiniest scale and make everything function.

For our understanding, quantum physics can be seen as the study of unseen principles that exist beyond space and time and how these impact our material, emotional, and spiritual reality here on Earth. As believers, we know that everything is a part of God's design, and forces beyond space and time influence and sustain this creation.

The order of creation works like this: God speaks an intention, which includes a specific design. The frequency of that design interacts with the creative essence of God's energy (which operates in quantum). When God says, "Let there be," the specific waveforms of the object being created move from the quantum realm into 3-D reality as they convert from waveforms to matter. Quantum contains God's creative presence where frequency blueprints are established holographically and then pass from waveform to matter on His command. When God speaks, creation happens instantaneously. When we are operating as co-creators it is by His word that we release into the quantum field.

Albert Einstein described one of these principles, called quantum entanglement, as "spooky action at a distance." This concept is demonstrated in an experiment where a person's blood was divided into two samples, with each half placed in different labs miles apart. One blood sample was stimulated with an electrical charge, and the technicians wanted to see if affecting one would influence the other. Surprisingly, not only did the distant sample respond, but it did so simultaneously with the one being stimulated. This unexpected result, known as "spooky action at a distance," showed how connected things can be, even across long distances.

For our purposes, we are exploring how principles that operate outside of space and time—like those in the quantum realm—can override the usual physical laws on Earth. Specifically, who or what can use the quantum grid, and at what level? How can quantum principles help us physically, emotionally, and spiritually? How is it interacted with? How does quantum affect our daily lives? Where is it described, and what are its actions in the Bible?

We will also discover that the quantum grid has an energy signature called scalar energy. We will learn more about frequencies and discover a process that starts with a thought in us that will eventually activate a response from the quantum grid. Ultimately, we will discover that our Heavenly Father allows us to interact with the grid to answer our assignment as co-creators with Him.

> *For [even the whole] creation [all nature] waits eagerly for the children of God to be revealed. (Romans 8:19, AMP)*

# Chapter 4
# The Wonders of Scalar Energy

For years, I've heard about scalar energy and its connection to quantum physics. Recently, I bought a device that operates using pure scalar energy and can even transmit specific frequencies from a Rife device into our physical bodies. To better understand how to use the device, I started studying scalar energy. As a child of the Most High, I began receiving revelation after revelation, as if Heaven gave me deeper insight. Here's what I've learned.

## Scalar Energy

Scalar energy is a part of God's complete bandwidth (energy, light, presence), which expresses His voice, holy fire, and energetic presence that designs, instructs, assembles, and holds all things together by His Word.

*And he is before all things, and by him all things consist (Colossians 1:17, KJV)*

## Scalar Energy Facts and Attributes

- **Restorative Power:** Pure energy is very restorative.
- **Connection to the Soul:** Scalar energy has a unique relationship to the human soul.
- **Field-Based, Not Point-Based**: Unlike other energies, scalar energy forms are based on the entire scalar energy field, not just from a single point.
- **Carries Information**: Scalar energy transmits information and creates geometric patterns.
- **Unaffected by Time and Distance**: Scalar energy doesn't weaken or lose its power over time or across distances.
- **Storage Beyond Space and Time**: Scalar energy can be stored in a dimension outside of our 3-D, carbon-based reality, ready to be released with a specific purpose—whether for healing, balance, or manifesting Heaven on Earth.
- **Divine Delivery System**: Scalar energy may be the system God uses to bring Heaven's design into reality on Earth.

- **Exclusive Access**: Only Yahweh and humanity have foundational access to scalar energy.

## Scalar Energy Interaction

Our personal DNA does more than just store functional and cellular data. It acts like an antenna, allowing us to access the vast information contained within the greater scalar energy field. Through this, humanity has a direct link to that immense informational resource.

We connect to this information by focusing our intention on specific topics or areas within the "scalar energy pool." When we form an intent, the energy generated by our thoughts reaches beyond the physical 3-D world into the higher scalar energy realm. Our brain does not inherently store scalar energy information; instead, it allows us to tap into scalar energy's vast informational resource pool, allowing our intention to transform from the unseen into the seen.

An interesting side effect of using our brain to create intent is that it also causes our body's cells to resonate with that intention. Our DNA amplifies this resonance, strengthening the energy field of intent as we reach out to the scalar energy realm.

Additionally, since the human body is 60-70% water, scalar energy has a powerful effect on us. Water can be influenced and programmed by scalar energy. As our intention is released, the water we hold in our body forms microclusters that resonate with the scalar energy, adding to the strength of the field needed to bring that which is unseen into 3-D reality, making us an interactive "scalar energy tool," so to speak.

I will emphasize this point several times: it appears that only the Creator and those made in His image have access to this deep interaction with the scalar energy field and its vast information. This unique access allows us to be co-creators with Yahweh, as we are meant to act in alignment with what we see Him do.

> *So Jesus answered them by saying, "I assure you and most solemnly say to you, the Son can do nothing of Himself [of His own accord], unless it is something He sees the Father doing; for whatever things the Father does, the Son [in His turn] also does in the same way." (John 5:19, AMP)*

What I have shared so far should prompt us to take this Proverb more seriously:

> *For as he thinks in his heart, so is he. (Proverbs 23:7)*

We should also regard James 3:1-12 with greater seriousness, as it instructs us about the power of the tongue. Both passages are significant because our words can trigger scalar energy interactions.

# Chapter 5
# Momentum

For our discussion, *momentum* refers to the time it takes for a thought to begin engaging with the quantum field. In the first seventeen seconds, if a thought is laid aside, nothing happens. From seventeen to sixty-eight seconds, we must learn to either stop that thought or let it build. Once we reach sixty-eight seconds, that thought starts the process of engaging with the quantum or scalar energy field (which I will explain later). It's important to remember that every thought we have has an impact, whether positive or negative. Plus, sixty-eight seconds is momentum.

## A Passing Thought

Our bodies are about seventy percent water, and the Earth is roughly seventy percent water. Scientists have conducted numerous experiments demonstrating that water can be programmed positively or negatively. Should the children of the Most High be speaking to the water on our planet? Those aligned with darkness do this regularly. As noted in Luke 16:8:

> *And the lord commended the unjust steward because he had done wisely: for the children of this world are in their generation wiser than the children of light. (KJV)*

We may be able to lessen the current negative influences if we speak positive words into lakes, rivers, and oceans. While I'm uncertain about the extent of our potential impact, we won't know until we try.

## What Humanity Shares

The concept of scalar energy includes elements of collective consciousness and collective memory. As humans, we all participate in these because we are connected to one of two opposing systems:

1. Tree of the Knowledge of Good and Evil.
2. Tree of Life.

While this idea doesn't imply a "hive mentality," it does illustrate our interconnectedness, whether we like it or not. This means that if we are connected to all of humanity, our ability to send blessings to others can have a much greater impact, even when it's difficult.

Given the way scalar energy works and because we are constantly interacting with it, we need to keep in mind that our words, thoughts, and emotions will affect others even if they are not physically present when we trigger a scalar energy interaction with our thoughts (intent) or with an emotional response.

James 3:1-12:

> [1] *Not many [of you] should become teachers [serving in an official teaching capacity], my brothers and sisters, for you know that we [who are teachers] will be judged by a higher standard [because we have assumed greater accountability and more condemnation if we teach incorrectly].* [2] *For we all stumble and sin in many ways. If anyone does not stumble in what he says [never saying the wrong thing], he is a perfect man [fully developed in character, without serious flaws], able to bridle his whole body and rein in his entire nature [taming his human faults and weaknesses].* [3] *Now, if we put bits into the horses' mouths to make them obey us, we guide their whole body as well.* [4] *And look at the ships. Even though they are so large and are driven by strong winds, they are still directed by a very small rudder, wherever the impulse of the helmsman*

*determines. ⁵ In the same sense, the tongue is a small part of the body, and yet it boasts of great things. See [by comparison] how great a forest is set on fire by a small spark! ⁶ And the tongue is [in a sense] a fire, the very world of injustice and unrighteousness; the tongue is set among our members as that which contaminates the entire body and sets on fire the course of our life [the cycle of man's existence], and is itself set on fire by hell (Gehenna). ⁷ For every species of beasts and birds, of reptiles and sea creatures, is tamed and has been tamed by the human race. ⁸ But no one can tame the human tongue; it is a restless evil [undisciplined, unstable], full of deadly poison. ⁹ With it we bless our Lord and Father, and with it we curse men, who have been made in the likeness of God. ¹⁰ Out of the same mouth come both blessing and cursing. These things, my brothers, should not be this way [for we have a moral obligation to speak in a manner that reflects our fear of God and profound respect for His precepts]. ¹¹ Does a spring send out from the same opening both fresh and bitter water? ¹² Can a fig tree, my brothers, produce olives, or a grapevine produce figs? Nor can salt water produce fresh. (AMP)*

This scalar energy interaction is so powerful that those who reach a level of proficiency can affect the weather. Scalar energy devices exist that are strong enough to cause earthquakes (i.e., those developed by Nikola Tesla).

> *There is more in the stars
> than what we know.*

It is quite possible that the stars we see at night shine because of the way the greater scalar energy system operates. They serve as glittering reminders of the endless possibilities within the Kingdom. Could it be that they, too, are longing for the revelation of the sons of God, just like other parts of creation?

## Filters and Static

While scalar energy may be how the unseen becomes seen (Hebrews 11:1-2), we must also remember that we have an enemy that is well aware of the mechanical side of how the scalar energy system and process works. Although the enemy may not be able to directly manipulate quantum energy, he will take every opportunity to create an environment that tempts us to speak words that release negative energy. This negative energy can be exploited to support his rebellious agenda.

> *¹ Now faith is the assurance (title deed, confirmation) of things hoped for (divinely guaranteed), and the evidence of things not seen [the conviction of their reality—faith comprehends as fact what cannot be experienced by the physical senses]. ² For by this [kind of] faith the men of old gained [divine] approval.* (Hebrews 11:1-2, AMP)

I stated earlier that Yahweh and humanity are the only ones who can access the fullness of scalar energy. It makes sense then that our enemy would like to keep us ignorant of our full birthright and potential once we are fully restored by being born from above. To do this, he ensures that his minions shoot continual chaotic frequencies in our direction until we become mature enough to resist.

The desired result of such "warfare" is that we will be forced to put our focus on health, finances, and emotional survival with the intent to keep us continually distracted! How dangerous would we be if we understood all of Heaven's potential resources and then became proficient in their use? Imagine that!

Imagine the sheer terror in the enemy's camp if even one believer realized that God's fire, glory, light, and living water can lead us to greater intimacy and personal balance. I refer to these as the *big four*. Should that person begin to engage in quantum, they might discover these things can be classified as weaponry.

The caveat is that even if we understand that these *big four* have multiple applications, should we engage these out of our own volition, we are still operating at the lower end of the quantum grid's bandwidth. Remember, Jesus only did what He saw the Father do. Should we allow the Father's emotional realm to be the driving force, we can transcend the limitations of electromagnetic frequencies and move into the realm of magneto-electric energy. This magneto-electric field includes what I call the "God factor." We will know we are in our "sweet spot" when the frequencies of our voice are fully harmonized with the frequencies of the Father's voice.

# Chapter 6
# The Way, the Truth, and the Life

While the church and Christianity often focus primarily on salvation, the bigger picture is that every human comes to Earth on assignment. Our main mission is to answer the groanings of creation and participate in restoring both the Earth and humanity. First, we need to be restored to our Father and welcomed back into the Family. After that, we can work through the personal issues such as legalities against us, trauma, filters, and the static that holds us back. As we grow in intimacy with Father's heart, we can begin to move into our personal assignment.

However, if we have not accepted God's approved channel of restoration, we are barred from the highest level of the scalar energy process. Therefore, due to original sin, we are then left to interact with the basic mechanics of scalar energy, often encountering lower or even destructive energy forms.

It's important to note that these lower energy forms can include Christianity as a mental or superficial practice, as well as various "isms" and all metaphysical expressions. I also have a deep concern about Christian teachings based on personal experiences that distort scripture to support them. I have tested the voiceprint of some of these people and the results are not encouraging. Be aware.

Let us be big boys and girls and not be empty-headed enough to put our wonderful light under a bushel and then go on thinking we are doing "God's work."

In my book *Moving Toward Sonship*, I encourage people to focus on resolving personal legalities, inner struggles, and emotional wounds before stepping into Kingdom work. If we move too quickly, we become vulnerable and may fall into false teachings that divert us from our true mission. None of us want to operate in confusion or mixed messages.

Scalar energy can take our intentions, release them into the quantum field, and connect them with spiritual substance to help us overcome physical, emotional, and traumatic issues. Be reminded that scalar energy can reach out into quantum essence (the material of creation) as a delivery system and bring us what we need to move toward greater wholeness.

## It Has Always Been About Him

We must remember that God (Yahweh) is the primal source of all light, design forms, waves, and frequencies. All light carries a frequency that can be traced, like an IP address back to its source. When Father said, "Let there be light," He was establishing scalar energy as universal intelligence and instruction. Therefore, scalar energy can design, instruct, assemble and hold things together. (Colossians 1:17) Scalar energy is essentially frequency (or code) embedded in light. All things were created in Him, by Him, and for Him. (Colossians 1:16)

Consider this example: When we look at the sun, we see only white light. However, when we hold up a prism, that light is split into seven colors—red, orange, yellow, green, blue, indigo, and violet. Interestingly, these are the same colors associated with the Seven Spirits of God. I wonder what role the Magnificent Seven plays in this process.

Humans also have an energy field around them, like a bubble that we walk in. That field displays seven distinct colors. Can you guess which seven colors they are? Each of these fields spins like a vortex and enhances our ability to engage with the scalar energy system—if we are redeemed. Regular intimate engagements with Father increase the strength of the frequencies each color carries.

On the other hand, those who haven't accepted Christ as Lord and Savior have a very limited ability to interact with scalar energy, and it remains mostly mechanical for them. It's like wearing 100 SPF sunscreen that blocks 99% of the sun's rays—only a small fraction gets through. If they are content with that 1%, imagine how much more we should appreciate having access to the full 100%!

---

*It's time to switch from s-u-n block to S-O-N life!*

---

## Back to the Brain

Think back to when computers stored everything directly on the device. Today, computers come with limited storage, just enough to access the cloud and handle tasks. Similarly, before the fall in Eden, humanity may have been more like those fully equipped computers. Now, we're more like modern computers, equipped with just enough to connect to the "cloud"—the vast spiritual resources available to us.

This is good for several reasons: first, it limits humans not born from above to how deeply they can go into scalar energy, and second, it keeps the true believer dependent on the Lord for spiritual growth.

The church has been so *salvation-focused* that little effort has been put into discovering what scientific modalities are available to help our growth and empower our walk with signs and wonders following. It's disheartening to consider that we have the Bible—a complete instruction manual—at our fingertips. The Bible is filled with layers of wisdom and revelation, offering the potential for an entirely new level of spiritual experience.

What's even more troubling is how Eastern mystics, from a misguided standpoint, have explored the mechanics of scalar energy while we, who have access to a much greater truth, often do nothing with it. This includes the exploration of what we might call "spiritual science."

# Chapter 7
# Only for the Bold

Those who embrace the whole message of God's Kingdom understand they must first clear the filters and distractions from being born under the effects of Adam and Eve's transgression. Sons also know they must align their realms (body, soul, and spirit) and daily bring their spirit forward. Remember, being born again fully restores our relationship with God and gives us access to Heaven's plans and resources.

Restoration doesn't mean we instantly know everything or understand all the resources available—especially at first. Implementing these plans is a good process because it allows us to confidently move forward without rushing ahead. Expanding our thinking is crucial to making progress. This process builds faith, which can be understood as *confident intention*.

## How does this work?

What if scalar energy is the scientific manifestation of God's love in action—His universal glue holding everything together? It's amusing that science is just now catching up to what God has placed around us all along.

In our physical reality, we move from point A to point B, but in the quantum realm, we think about it and are there! The difference between how the material and spiritual realms work is significant in function. Maybe it's time to create a quantum platform to source our physical needs directly from scalar energy, which ultimately comes from God's love and the entire design He desires for us to operate in.

## How do we enter this scalar energy (quantum) field?

- Prayer automatically puts us into quantum—we just need to be more aware of what happens when we pray.
- Worship connects us to quantum.
- Bringing our spirit forward does the same.

- Being seated with Christ in heavenly places means we're always in quantum; we simply need to become more aware of it.
- Intentional thoughts connect us with scalar energy reality—our mind is a scalar energy vessel.
- We should become more aware of how our intention affects our DNA and the water in our bodies.
- Practice raising the melody of each realm so that they combine into a symphony, which allows us to directly interact with scalar energy.

These are all ways we can continually interact with scalar energy. We need to make this mindset our new normal. We also need to get with God's program and quit letting the limited design of planet Earth dictate our reality.

## A Necessary Ingredient

As we expand our understanding of reality to match God's design, we must also recognize the role of **faith.**

It seems likely that the Lord is revealing the mysteries of universal mechanics (how the universe works) at this time in history to help us build confidence as we boldly go where few in Christianity have dared to go. Faith, as "confident intention," helps us engage with the unseen realm, knowing we're not just experimenting without purpose.

Following the Lord Jesus' example of only doing what we see the Father doing as we step into an assignment or engagement helps us know that what we do is more than real.

If we set an intention with faith, we activate our quantum link, which establishes a holographic structure outside of space and time. By confidently releasing faith into that structure, we can trust that it will eventually manifest on Earth.

It is also helpful to know that the reason we use speech (as opposed to telepathy) on Earth is that the theater of operations we are in is designed to respond to the frequencies and intent expressed in our speech.

## Let's Look at Some More Examples

Many of us are familiar with going to heavenly courts to reverse generational or personal legalities, but what about engaging in restoration and repayment, knowing there's an interactive field waiting to help us?

After receiving a mandate from God, we release it into Earth. With the scalar energy process, we can check beyond space and time to see its progress. Is there a holographic structure forming in the scalar energy field? Does it need more faith? It's comforting to know we can do this.

What about physical illness? Sometimes, lack of knowledge or spiritual legalities opens doors for the enemy to send harmful frequencies that manifest as symptoms or diseases. According to John 10:10, all diseases come from darkness. While we should acknowledge a diagnosis, we're free to reject it as the final word.

Any health crisis is an opportunity to formulate our intention to react with scalar energy and create a construct of health in the quantum field. Remember, quantum is in the realm outside of time and space. When we release faith, a scalar energy surge comes into our body. This overwrites carbon reality with a higher spiritual reality, this time with the energy of God's love and His higher plan.

James 4:2:

*You do not have because you do not ask [it of God].*
*(AMP)*

What about cosmic or planetary chaos? While it's not something most of us think about, could it benefit Earth if stars and planets affected by the great rebellion were restored to sing their songs again? What if Father waits for us to volunteer for a cosmic assignment that brings such restoration? What if God waits for us to take on cosmic assignments that bring restoration? Remember, only Yahweh, you, and I are authorized to interact with scalar energy at this level.

What about people who took the COVID-19 vaccine? Are you willing to ask God for an assignment to help them? By setting your intention, you could build a supercharged holographic solution and, by faith, release it to them. Since space, time, and distance don't matter, why not release nonphysical scalar energy into their situation with complete confidence?

## A Bit of Perspective

John 17:14:

*They are not of the world, even as I am not of the world. (KJV)*

Could this verse mean more than we realize? The whole purpose of this book is to challenge people to expand their thinking to the point that ALL that God has for us is something each of us can seek out and walk in. However, to walk in this fullness, we must learn to do it God's way, which may be different from what we've been taught in the past.

We've often been taught that heavenly integration happens mostly after we die. But what if God expects more from us now? The infrastructure is already in place for us to experience more of Heaven now.

I have pointed out that God has put in place a tangible, although invisible, system where we can utilize the very energy of God's love to call nearly everything around us to a much higher purpose. And we get to help put it in place!

The energy we feel when God's presence comes, the power that flows when we lay hands on someone, or even the energy that healed the woman who touched Jesus' garment—it all comes from the Father's heart and His love. There is a system in place for us to access and release this energy into situations and to others.

Understanding scalar energy gives us much greater confidence. It shows us that we can be in multiple places and address many issues without physically moving. There's a divine energy platform surrounding us, just waiting for anyone who calls on God's name to engage it.

# Chapter 8
# Quantum Has a Designed Mechanical Side

Everything God creates has design, purpose, and mechanics, which can be understood as divine order. This order doesn't lose value if God chooses to reveal how parts of it work. Take angels, for example. From our perspective, they are supernatural beings. However, from their perspective, all they do and how they operate is entirely normal to them.

In the grand scheme, all things are part of God's creation, but not every part follows the same rules. On Earth, it appears there are operational limits in place. When someone or something comes from a realm without those limitations or different ones, it may seem supernatural to us.

How surprising would it be to learn that beings, like angels, could become visible to us simply by adjusting their frequency to match Earth's limits? This adjustment would allow us to see them with our natural eyes. The same concept could apply to objects.

For example, when Jesus told Peter to catch a fish and found a coin in its mouth, did the fish eat a coin someone had dropped, or did the coin supernaturally appear from Heaven and manifest on Earth? Similarly, how did the loaves and fishes multiply? *I am starting to understand that faith activates a system that's already in place rather than just engaging with empty space, hoping somehow something will happen.*

Part of "on Earth, as it is in Heaven" likely refers to more than just godly behaviors. I am sure it refers to God's government and the way all things operate outside the restraints this part of the cosmos is locked into. What are those ways? Should we expect more visible manifestations from those of us who live in both Heaven and Earth at the same time? After all, this is part of a quantum reality.

I asked Father a pointed question. "Father, how much of quantum is a part of the fabric of creation, and how much comes from You directly?" He told me that only the Godhead and mankind are designed to address the creative side of quantum. And then He answered that thirty-five percent is woven into creation, and sixty-five percent comes directly from Him. Time will tell how accurate these numbers are, but they open up exciting possibilities.

For example, the misuse of electromagnetic principles in quantum, like using voice activation to attract things for selfish reasons outside of God's guidance, can be seen in ideas like "The Secret" and the law of attraction. This also includes witchcraft, voodoo, and other mystical practices not approved by God.

Sadly, some believers with a measure of discernment have noticed such misappropriation of resources and have thrown the baby out with the bath water. Having ultimately dismissed the mechanical side that responds to any human, saved or unsaved, that person will say any interaction with quantum is "New Age" or even evil.

## A Prophetic Word on the Subject

(This word was given to me personally by the Lord.)

*Know that when Adam and Eve fell, they fell from being able to fully interact with how I designed all creation to be an interactive "living fabric" of creative life that completes its circle by lifting praise to Me.*

*Your enemy is fully unplugged from any life-giving system in my designs of creation, and there are many. In fact, they are (the enemy) very limited and are only allowed in certain areas, and they delight in occupying territory that I intended for my children to govern.*

*I could have eliminated those of the Great Rebellion; however, as initial punishment, I chose to limit them in many ways and put them with those limitations in an area they were once in charge of. That area is planet Earth and the surrounding cosmos, which would bear the consequences of their rebellion. And that is where I put Adam and Eve right in the middle as my testimony.*

*For any realm to exist there still is an "existence" design. This means some level of quantum will be present. Because their realm's design is so limited, the evil leaders plotted to find a way to boost their system to maintain a measure of what they had lost. The main motive to get Adam and Eve to fall was so they could steal some of mankind's "light" and use what they could for their evil purposes. One could observe that even though their realm could be made to look like an entire alternative realm, in reality, it was and is nothing but smoke and mirrors playing off of mankind's authority.*

*To maintain their "smoke and mirrors," their way to tap into mankind's authority is through the New Age, Satanism, Universalism, Eastern Mysticism, and the like. All of this is focused on creating chaos and trauma and robbing mankind of their emotional strength to fuel their system while hurting the apple of my eye in the process.*

We see where the battle is. (Ephesians 6:12) Yes, the lower frequencies of the quantum can be used by the unsaved and those born from above as long as a person is fully human.

# Chapter 9
# Expanded Thinking

You will hear more about the need to expand your thinking, and here's why: the truth we've accepted as "normal" in our minds is only part of the bigger story. As believers, we are seated with Christ Jesus in heavenly places (Ephesians 2:1, 4-7). We are called to do even greater things than Jesus did (John 14:12-14). We are spiritually connected to our Creator (John 14:20) and tasked with addressing Creation's groaning (Romans 8:19). To accomplish this, we can't keep thinking the same way or repeating the same actions while expecting different results. It's time to find out how to align with God's way.

> [1] *And you [He made alive when you] were [spiritually] dead and separated from Him because of your transgressions and sins....*

> *⁴ But God, being [so very] rich in mercy, because of His great and wonderful love with which He loved us, ⁵ even when we were [spiritually] dead and separated from Him because of our sins, He made us [spiritually] alive together with Christ (for by His grace—His undeserved favor and mercy—you have been saved from God's judgment). [Rom 6:1-10] ⁶ And He raised us up together with Him [when we believed], and seated us with Him in the heavenly places, [because we are] in Christ Jesus, ⁷ [and He did this] so that in the ages to come He might [clearly] show the immeasurable and unsurpassed riches of His grace in [His] kindness toward us in Christ Jesus [by providing for our redemption]. (Ephesians 2:1,4-7 AMP)*

I do not doubt that understanding quantum mechanics, particularly the energy system known as scalar energy waves, is important for us to understand and start engaging with it. You don't need to be a quantum physicist to grasp enough of it to build confidence in interacting with quantum principles.

Hopefully, I've provided enough background for you to feel confident that this system is something we can tap into as we're led. Now, we need examples of how to engage. Let's look at a few more foundational quantum principles before diving into how to engage with it:

- The quantum field retains the memory of everything we say, feel, and do—whether positive or negative.
- Frequencies (or waveforms) determine the look and physicality of an object.
- If we could match the waveform of a solid object, we could pass our hand through it, as its atoms are ninety percent empty space.
- Quantumly entangled photons resemble the Yin Yang symbol.
- Quantum is voice-activated based on the quality and design of the frequencies contained in the human voice.

In quantum mechanics, all possibilities exist in the present. However, our brains are programmed by 3-D Earth limitations to view the future based on past experiences—essentially, how we've been taught things work. This limits us from changing the present because the patterns of the past block our ability to positively impact both the present and future. This is true primarily because we are limited by what we think. Let me remind you that our brain's function in quantum is to turn intention into a frequency, not to act as a barrier.

To engage with quantum principles, we must first recognize that we all have a personal energy field. When we react to someone or something (like news), we draw from our energy field, and our reaction turns that news into chemistry. When this happens, the field around us shrinks, making us more matter and less energy, with more particles and fewer waves. When we operate more as "matter" than energy, we try to force the outcome or control it. Being more physical prevents us from engaging quantum and activating its design. Essentially, we remove ourselves from the possibility of catching a fish with the coin in its mouth.

Some time ago, when the Father began to speak to me about His quantum heart and emotional realms, He told me that His emotional realm was far more than just emotions—it carries creative designs, which I didn't fully understand at first. It is His emotional realm that helps us maintain an elevated energy field around us. As we increase our intimacy with the Father, His presence resonates within us like a tuning fork used to tune an instrument. Quality time with Father equips us to fully engage quantum and, therefore, engage our co-creative assignments. And as His emotions become ours, we discover that emotional energy is a powerful activator in the quantum realm.

Proximity in relationship helps us remain more as frequency (waveform) than physical matter. The result is that we will have an elevated energy field of up to twenty-nine feet. It might sound unbelievable because we're not used to thinking this way, but there are examples of this power in Scripture. One such example is when the shadow of the Apostles passed over people, and they were healed.

> *Insomuch that they brought forth the sick into the streets, and laid them on beds and couches, that at the least the shadow of Peter passing by might overshadow some of them. (Acts 5:15, KJV)*

There is a remarkable story I know of a lady who was doing dishes and worshipping at the same time. The lady's mom came in to say something to her and freaked out because the level of worship she was engaged in caused her to become almost transparent. The possibilities are quite intriguing.

When we are more energy than matter, the possibility of manifesting heavenly mandates and the promises of God's Word in physical reality grows exponentially. The results we will see are directly in proportion to our level of intimacy with the Father. At that level, no one can fake it. This is the 65% of Father's presence that is only available to believers. If we can sustain a higher waveform long enough then we can broadcast an intentional blueprint directly into the quantum essence realm. This realm is where the invisible substance of creation is. (Hebrews 11:1-2)

Faith comes in as the electrical charge, while feelings (emotions) provide the magnetic charge that results in an electromagnetic signature to our cells that turns us into a quantum interface with the quantum field as we rise above Earth's limitations. It is the "voice" that triggers the magneto-electric signature of quantum so it will manifest in Earth's reality. This is what the "new age" has stolen from us: God's creative design for us to be co-creators as long as we <u>only do</u> what we see Him do. (John 5:19)

## The Process

- **Receive an Idea or Promise:** Begin with an idea from the Father or a promise from His Word to establish your intention.
- **Internalize It:** Take this idea into your heart, where it begins to take shape. This is where the birthing takes place.
- **Amplify the Intention:** Send the energized idea to your brain, which transforms it into a waveform, magnifying its intent.
- **Activate Your DNA:** The frequency generated triggers your DNA to cooperate, releasing the

frequency into the water within your cells, turning you into an interactive quantum broadcast center.
- **Speak with Faith:** Use your voice, combined with faith in the Father's emotional design, to broadcast into God's quantum creative essence. This action activates the full potential of quantum, enabling a process where Heaven can manifest on Earth from a source beyond the confines of space and time.

The first step in this five-step process is to enter into the Father's heart. As we stand in His heart, *He feels what we feel*. We are also standing amid His Quantum Emotional Realm by standing in His heart. In that moment, He resonates with what we bring to Him. In this space, we may also receive assignments or mandates from Him. Then, as His heart reaches out to touch our heart, that environment brings His emotional design into the matter. He is tuning us to His higher design on multiple levels.

That emotional exchange becomes the spark we need as we prepare to verbalize our co-creative release into the quantum grid. Intention combined with His emotion adds incredible power as we impart frequency design into the quantum grid. This grid serves as a bridge for heavenly designs to manifest on Earth, transforming spiritual wavelengths into visible reality—not because it's solely our idea, but because we are releasing what we observe the Father doing (John 5:19). The key here is that God gives the plan and we speak it to anchor it in the quantum field. God responds in measure to the quality of what we release so it will manifest on Earth.

If you find this hard to believe, remember that what I've outlined here reflects what we've been unconsciously doing throughout our lives, often with adverse outcomes. Now that we recognize these repetitive cycles, it's time to break free. Remember that momentum begins after sixty-eight seconds, whether we want it to or not!

*In retrospect, I wonder how much of what we have blamed on the Devil was actually just our words interacting with the quantum field. Then, we sit back, complain, and wait for God to intervene in problems we have created ourselves.*

This system operates whether we acknowledge it or not; it was designed to respond to both God and humanity. Therefore, if someone continually expresses a victim mentality, they will likely attract similar issues into their lives. The Bible refers to this as the principle of sowing and reaping, a fundamental aspect of God's created order:

*Do not be deceived, God is not mocked [He will not allow Himself to be ridiculed, nor treated with contempt nor allow His precepts to be scornfully set aside]; for whatever a man sows, this and this only is what he will reap. ⁸ For the one who sows to his flesh [his sinful capacity, his worldliness, his disgraceful impulses] will reap from the flesh ruin and destruction, but the one who sows to the Spirit will from the Spirit reap eternal life. (Galatians 6:7-8, AMP)*

# Chapter 10
# Let's Plug in Some Examples

We must remember that we have two sources for our intentions: (1) God's Word and (2) specific guidance He provides, which will always align with His Word. His Word is a reliable foundation we can draw at any time.

For instance, if finances are low, you can turn to the Word to secure God's promise of provision for the vision He has given you. You take the scriptures and hide them in your heart (your thinking center). Be aware that there may need to be an incubation period. Once you know the time has come to enable a state of change, you add confidence (faith) to your intention.

As you direct that intention to your brain, it generates an electromagnetic frequency that activates your DNA antennae, which in turn energizes your cells so that your electromagnetic field moves out toward the desired twenty-nine feet.

At this point, you become more wave than matter so that when you speak the intention out in faith, your voice triggers the magneto-electric properties of quantum (scalar energy).

This process starts with God and, because of our involvement, returns to Him, completing a circle. This circle becomes a shield that blocks chaos and resistance, allowing only blessing and new life. Restoration is about re-establishing the fullness of the relationship with all things. While co-creation can be something totally new, it can also upgrade the object of our focus, restoring the song or purpose to the object of our assignment.

We can apply this sequence to address any needs we have, whether we are working through all the filters and static hindering us or implementing Kingdom mandates.

Consider the following:

- Unifying our body, soul, and spirit.
- Maximizing the potential of our DNA.
- Transforming our DNA.
- Seeing, knowing, hearing, and feeling better as we engage God.

- Upgrade our heart and emotional realms to match Father's design.
- Be more aware of what diminishes our frequency field and practice building it out.
- We activate aspects of our scroll into the quantum realm and then bring them into Earth reality.
- Recognizing that if we ever translocate, we must be more wave than matter.

In all this, we are developing skills and spiritual maturity to walk as bonafide sons and daughters of the Most High. Creation eagerly awaits our engagement!

Another essential principle based on quantum reality is this:

---
*We are not punished **for** our sins.*
*We are punished **by** our sins!*

---

It is a simple case of cause and effect. This is the cycle we inherited from Adam and Eve. However, being born from above is the ultimate and only true realignment that can break this cycle. Knowing Jesus is the only way to break this cycle and the only way to move our personal energy field to a full twenty-nine feet. Any other way will not work. The frequencies will not be there for the gates to open, as the necessary frequencies won't align for quantum to respond.

Now, do you see why the enemy is intent on keeping us dumbed down and wallowing in repetitive generational cycles of sin and mental blockages? He knows what a true son or daughter of the King is capable of. The question is: do we?

Salvation is far more than just a ticket to Heaven; it comes packaged with the potential for an unsurpassable personal restoration that moves us into a frequency zone where we can:

- Fully demonstrate the Kingdom to restore others.
- Restore creation.
- Have access to incredible heavenly resources.
- Live on Earth and Heaven simultaneously (Ephesians 2:6).
- Be in multiple places simultaneously (a quantum reality).
- Have full access to the very heart and mind of God.
- Be restored to family DNA so we can resonate and be tuned by the Father.

## Let us Talk About the Tongue

Our voice is more than merely sound; it acts as a trigger for scalar energy/quantum energy. Sound can carry loads of information. I utilize the information in a person's voice to make my nutritional and spiritual testing assessments. I have been doing this for over 30 years with incredible accuracy.

If my mechanical testing cannot be deceived, I believe that quantum systems operate under similar principles, remaining impervious to deception. In the spirit realm, the frequencies we embody function like biometric identification devices as we present ourselves in different realms or as we attempt to engage quantum. This indicates that the frequency signature of intention is present in every word we utter at any level. Remember, in quantum, like attracts like, so **we can only rise to the frequency of what we carry within ourselves.** Quantum both recognizes and responds to the level of authenticity we carry.

*For as he thinks in his heart, so is he. (Proverbs 23:7, AMP)*

Quantum's mode of operation with scalar energy is designed to respond to like frequencies. This interaction completes the cycle of Creation as praise returns to the

Father. This is the law of sowing and reaping in demonstration.

Quantum essence, as the fundamental substance of creation, flows through the quantum grid and can store memory. This means every word we say has the potential to be stored as memory. Because this has positive and negative connotations, we must be mindful of every word we say, even if said in jest. This is what the Apostle James warned us about—the power of the tongue.

I recommend taking some time and purposely rescinding all the words you have said that would not serve a purpose in the quantum grid. Additionally, purposefully release blessings to the quantum grid to be used by you at a later date and to make them available to others.

I suggest taking time and purposely rescinding any negative words you may have released into the quantum field. You could say something like this;

> *As a son of the Most High God I rescind any words I may have released into the quantum field from a position of frustration or any other selfish reason. I direct that these words and any accompanying intention be removed from the quantum field and that they will be as if they never were.*

I also suggest that from now on, you direct your efforts toward speaking blessings into the quantum grid for your family and anything that you know relates to your personal assignment.

Our Heavenly Father set the precedent in the very first verse of the Bible, where it says,

*In the origin (in Genesis), God (Elohim) brought into existence out of nothing the skies and the earth.*

This is a literal translation by a Hebrew scholar. While you and I are not assigned to this level of creation, we are assigned to reconciliation. To fulfill such an assignment, we will have to operate outside of space and time as we utilize the quantum grid. A grid designed to respond to faith, intention, and heavenly blueprints just waiting to be activated by you and me.

# Chapter 11
# The Song of Our Realms

Years ago, the Lord spoke to me and said, "You know you have a personal song." At the time, I didn't realize that our DNA has its own melody, but I sensed it could be more significant than I understood. Over the years, I've learned that our body, soul, and spirit each have their own songs, and when we are united with ourselves and with the Lord, these three combine to create a beautiful symphony.

While I appreciated the importance of this union, I didn't fully grasp the purpose of our songs until I began to explore quantum principles. Our songs help complete the creative praise cycle that returns to the Lord as well as allowing us to maintain our energy field at a very high level. Remember, this keeps us more waveform than matter so we can actively engage in the quantum field.

## Achieving Greater Union

To achieve a deeper union, we must clear out generational legalities, traumas, filters, and static. Once this is achieved, when we engage God's presence through prayer and worship, we position ourselves for the free flow of His glory, fire, light, and living water. Our songs help us maintain that flow *and* release it as needed.

## My Testing Protocols

Our voices contain a wealth of information. Included in that information are the following that I can test for. Most are rated on a scale of 0-10, with ten being optimal.

- Union with the Lord.
- Union of body, soul, spirit.
- Level of the Quantum Emotional Realm.
- Level of Quantum Heart Realm.
- Level of Quantum Essence Realm.
- How well you see, hear, know, and feel.
- The level of fire, glory, light, and living water you maintain.
- Presence of negative detractors, including trauma.

I encourage anyone wanting to identify background noise in their lives to undergo my testing to pinpoint their specific detractors. Removing these obstacles allows us to expand our personal energy field to the sonship level.

## Summary

We need to begin living and demonstrating what Heaven considers normal, rising above the limited expectations of our 3-D earthly experience.

Key insights learned so far:

- A new branch of science exists that is not grounded in the linear electromagnetic paradigm.
- The properties of quantum, such as being outside of space and time and quantum entanglement, appear to be "supernatural."
- The quantum grid is voice-activated and operates on magneto-electric principles.
- Only God and humanity have full access to the key aspects of the quantum grid.
- All evil operates within the lower 1% of the grid and often with human agreement.
- All creation is sound (frequency) and light-based.
- In the quantum realm, we can share the properties of frequencies if we align ourselves with them.

- God's energy always restores and often brings a higher design or purpose.
- Through magneto-electric principles, our words have the power to harm or bless others.
- Believers shouldn't be intimidated by the fact that unbelievers can operate in the lower 1% of the quantum grid—this doesn't invalidate the rest of quantum's divine potential. Don't throw the baby out with the bathwater!
- The quantum field can store information, is a communication grid, and even has a level of consciousness because it is part of God's bandwidth, holding all creation together by His word.
- Higher aspects of quantum/scalar energy only respond to pure, high-level frequencies.
- Most spiritual warfare is designed to keep us distracted, preventing us from discovering the quantum grid and its divine purpose.
- Warfare also aims to keep our cells and organs out of balance, so we remain more material than wave, which blocks us from fully engaging with the quantum realm.
- The 5-step process of quantum engagement places a holographic blueprint in the quantum field, awaiting

conversion into 3-D reality by faith and the sound of our voice.
- You and I can become more wave than matter if we intentionally work at it, expanding our personal energy field up to twenty-nine feet.
- God's emotional realm, combined with faith, are critical factors in converting quantum waveforms into tangible, earthly matter.
- As we practice being more wave than matter, we can use our imagination as a viewing screen to monitor our progress.
- The only limitations are the ones we impose on ourselves regarding how much of Heaven we allow into our hearts to accomplish our full assignment.

**Our Assignment Includes:**

1. Restoring others
2. Restoring geographical areas
3. Restoring earthly governments
4. Restoring earthly economies
5. Restoring education
6. Restoring healthcare

7. Receiving heavenly revelations for breakthrough inventions and more.

With this understanding, our confidence should be limitless—knowing the Lord has created a vast system to activate His Word and His plans in our lives and here on Earth.

The real question is simple: Are you willing to allow your thinking to fully align with a more expansive heavenly truth? Will you allow the Holy Spirit to mentor you into the place where the fullness of quantum reality is your new normal?

Do you hear Creation crying out to you?

# Chapter 12
# Conclusion

Quantum, scalar energy, and Kingdom principles are nearly interchangeable, living concepts that we must learn to engage if we are to be true representatives of our King and our homeland (Heaven). There has likely never been a greater need than now for God's sons and daughters to rise. We must reflect our King with purity, demonstrating His Kingdom with precision and power.

To rise up, we must become people of no reputation, wholly lost in our love for Him. Love is, and always has been, the driving force and key to unlocking the blessings of God. Love is also the purest form of energy, the very glue of the quantum realm. It is the highest frequency. Without love, we are left operating at lower frequencies, relying solely on human abilities and willpower. Without love, we are nothing more than a sounding gong or a clanging cymbal. Genuine, selfless love and intimacy with the Lover of your soul are the requirements for entering into sonship and exercising quantum changes on the Earth. Quantum will not respond in the higher levels without His love flowing through us with rivers of living water.

My wife and I find great joy in spending time together. It doesn't have to be anything special—just moments each day where we focus entirely on each other. One of our favorite times is sitting on our screened back porch in the evenings as the intense south Alabama sun begins to fade. We sip sweet tea and talk. We enjoy each other's company, and even when we're apart, we're never far from each other's thoughts. However, as wonderful as that relationship is, it can't compare to the depth of intimacy I experience when I choose to spend uninterrupted time with the Lover of my soul, the Father.

When I sit with Him, free from distractions, He speaks to me, and I speak to Him. I step into His heart—my place of rest. If something is weighing on me, like the need for a lost loved one, ***I immediately begin to FEEL what HE feels for them*** because I am already in His quantum emotional realm. His pure emotional flow trumps mine every time, and that flow of love empowers me with His frequency. From there I can "speak creatively" to the situation. *This* is the launching pad for walking in even greater works than Jesus did. Intimacy and close friendship with the Godhead is essential. When the songs of my realms merge with the flow of the Father's heart for the need at hand, then the co-creative emotional charge that I can release into quantum is powerful—like comparing a firecracker to a hydrogen bomb.

Focus on getting to know Him deeper than you ever have before. As your relationship grows, the truths of this book will begin to fall into place, and you will witness wonders as you fulfill your heavenly destiny as a **son** of the Living God!

# Appendix A

## The Relationship Between God's Breath, Light, Fire, & Glory in Creation

*(This teaching is shared to strengthen your foundation on how our voice and the "Big Four" help in our quantum engagements.)*

Man was made from the dust of the Earth, and since the Earth itself was framed by God's Word, our makeup retains a quantum connection to the Creator. However, the fall introduced an inversion in the functional order of how God designed us—how He framed our total being. This inversion significantly diminished the flow of that quantum connection.

Being born from above, we are positioned to restore that flow fully. First, Christ in us—the hope of Glory—opens a direct pathway to His image and His name. Second, as we release faith while we engage the Living Word, we understand it revitalizes our diminished quantum link. Moreover, our personal star may act like a hyperbolic chamber, imparting personal resources and blueprints into our spirit under the category of the mysteries of God. These are the mysteries of God at work, designed to build and restore us as we grow in confidence, increasingly conform to His image, and demonstrate His name.

**Our personal star is a heavenly resource[2] in the third Heaven where the specific resources for our earthly assignment are stored and where we can quantumly visit for rest and refreshment.**

God's breath was imparted to Adam, and after that, he became a living soul. Indeed, that breath contained light, fire, glory, and perhaps more. God's breath into Adam was the substantive expression of the record that His light contains. Being made in God's image and likeness means we

---

[2] Kingdom Dynamics, Volume 1, by Dr. Ron M. Horner. LifeSpring Publishing, 2022. Page 235.

have abilities from above that should mirror His. Indicating that our breath should do the same things.

To be more specific, light contains the record of the Creator's design plans. Once light is released toward quantum essence, a being or thing materializes (light and frequency are in the voice). That imparted light also activates quantum essence in us and strengthens our quantum link to the Lord, which is how our design and function are maintained. Clearly, this applied to Adam in fullness before the fall. After the fall the strength and maintained flow of the quantum link became compromised when dark energy was introduced into the equation.

*Speaking of breath*, we must currently take a breath before we speak to release sound (voice) that contains frequency and often intention. As we do, we take in oxygen. I wonder if Adam needed oxygen to live before the fall or if God's imparted breath (light) and Adam's quantum connection were his source of life. We assume that because things are currently carbon-based, this has always been the case.

It seems clear to me that the fall caused man and perhaps all of Earth life to switch from a **light-based existence** to an **elemental-based** existence. An elemental-based existence would be subject to the *forces of darkness* and all the corruptive factors that go along with that darkness. Physically, man went from a being with an unlimited light and energy source to a being that could now wear out and die.

With the assignment of Adam still in place, man would now manifest lower light frequencies and even darkness through the mechanism within (soul) that once allowed mankind to be purveyors of God's pure light and all it contains. Man now **resonates** with **darkness** as a **default setting** rather than his original design of light.

**Being born from above** indeed restores relationships; however, in what way does this position us to return to our original state? By application, it is obvious that we are not instantly restored to Adam's pre-fall state when we accept Christ as Lord and Savior. We may further deduct that if full restoration is possible, it must be incrementally based, resulting from personal encounters with God and His word. Scientifically speaking, such encounters would gradually replace corrupted inner frequency wave patterns with higher heavenly designs. The result would be to increase our capacity to synchronize with and release all Heaven has to offer.

The *general church world* sees making it to Heaven as the end goal. But what if Heaven is just the starting point to deeper realms and deeper mysteries and secrets? If this is so, then we need to fully embrace this process because it would move us out of the theoretical to the verifiably material.

Adam's three-part nature was inverted at the fall. The opposite of inversion is a "direct relationship." In either case, the human soul is the central figure in both pictures. This is because the soul empowers what the flesh is connected to or empowers the record that the human spirit is connected to. *Clearly, this is a critical point of understanding.*

My observation is that our soul (inner flame) was designed to resonate with God's eternal heavenly flame in Heaven so that we become the representative of that flame on Earth. *"On Earth as it is in Heaven."* A reminder that we are made in His image and likeness.[3]

Let me be very clear: **being like Him** doesn't take away from His **preeminence.** Instead, He brings us into union with Himself so that we may reflect His likeness but not become Him. Consider the four faces of the heavenly cherubim—one

---

[3] See Genesis 1:27, and Romans 8:29.

of them is the face of a man! This reminds us that God, in His love, chose to include humanity in His divine family.

**Let's explore "fire" further.** The "fire" mentioned in being baptized in the Holy Spirit and Fire (Matthew 3:11) really speaks of a molecular change from one form to another. That's what fire does. In this case, it is to repurpose our being to once again reflect the light of our Creator into the Earth's realm. Perhaps we all need a deeper revelation and more interaction with God's holy fire.

Additionally, we need our inner light to continue growing and illuminating the Kingdom's secrets and mysteries. It's important to remember that mysteries are to be sought out, and secrets are in God's darkness, waiting for our light to shine on them. Inquiring in these two areas and allowing what we uncover to be absorbed into our being is all part of our growth process. Then, we put it into action as we are directed.

As we engage in the overall discovery and restoration process, we must recognize that Father has placed help stations in the fabric of creation on Earth and in the unseen realms. A case in point would be our star, which I mentioned previously, and how our DNA serves as an antenna to link the twelve gates[4] within our being to those found in Heaven.

Imagine the twelve gates in Heaven, with our spirit in the middle and our physical body containing the twelve earthly gates. If visualized, it would resemble a DNA structure, with our spirit located at the center, with the capacity to flow in both heavenly and earth directions. In essence, this is a picture of Jacob's ladder, connecting Heaven and Earth.

Again, the purpose is to build us line upon line so we may restore creation's original order in us and around us as we impart new heavenly concepts when our Father assigns them.

## Summary

When Adam and Eve fell, they lost their quantum link to the special intimacy and to the eternal life they once shared with God. Their body's energy source shifted from being light-based to element-based. As a result, they lost both their intimate relationship with God and their ability to impart Heaven's design to the world around them. Adam must have

---

[4] See Revelation 21.

been devastated once he realized the magnitude of what he had done.

To restore humanity's lost relationship and abilities, God sent His only Son to die in our place. This was the only approved cosmic-level act that could bring about that restoration. No other religious practice or philosophy holds the power for such redemption. This is why Jesus declared that He is the way, the truth, and the life and that no one can return to the Father except through Him—no exceptions, no alternatives.

In His mercy and grace Father has provided resources such as His Word and help stations that are available to restore intimacy, relationship, life source, and assignment to the level displayed in the person of His only Son. We are called to be like Him, though not to become Him.

Being like Him means we share His DNA, attributes, voice, and behaviors if we press into the depths of His heart. This is the true meaning of intimacy with God—a profound quantum entanglement at its highest level. That's our story and His.

# Appendix B

## How Gemstones Can Help Our Walk

### Why Gemstones?

**Scientific Truth:**

- Most bodily functions are hormonally driven at some point.
- Vitamins and minerals nurture the body and provide raw materials the body needs for hormonal and cellular functions.
- However, is it the raw materials and our various hormones that do the work, or is it really the frequencies they carry?

If these elements emit frequencies, it stands to reason that the best-quality frequencies would come from the highest-quality materials.

**Question:** What happens when the quality of our diet is compromised or if we're exposed to environmental toxins?

**Answer:** Lower quality frequencies, which in turn can lead to disease.

## What Doc has to say:

I prefer gemstone medallions over frequency patches and essential oils because they last longer over time and don't need to be repurchased. Medallions never wear out and only need to be recharged by putting them in direct sunlight from time to time.

Each gemstone emits a specific frequency that can benefit our well-being, but many people are unaware of the effects these frequencies can have. I've researched to ensure that each medallion operates according to its intended purpose.

The medallions that I have designed fall into two categories: some are wellness-focused, and some are designed to buffer emotional and spiritual static so you can gain an edge as you seek greater intimacy with God.

The rectangle-shaped ones are 2"x 1". The largest "Unlocking 3-D Reality" is 2-3/4" diameter.

## Gemstones as Frequency Boosters

Since the beginning of humanity, mankind has used gemstones as adornments and a sign of wealth, power, and position. Scripture describes how gemstones serve as building materials in Heaven, but could that be their only purpose? Science has discovered that our cells contain crystalline structures, including the pineal gland with its microscopic crystals. Nicola Tesla once noted that crystals exhibit "living being" properties, with potential uses for sending and receiving frequencies.

Most of humanity gets up every morning without pondering how the universe or creation's fabric is constructed. But just as a light switch is assumed to work, few consider the complexities that make it so. For some, the focus shifts from "Why are we here?" to exploring what surrounds us and how it operates.

Scripture reveals that what is seen and unseen was created by God's spoken Word and empowered by His light. Creation is ordered and kept in order by His Word, and light is its power source, being a part of His essence. He is light, and things are and can be made (of) by light. In that light are countless bits of information, much like that which is carried by fiber optic cables. This tells me that creation may not be static but an ongoing process as His light continually engages the foundational substance of creation that He left in place.

In a perfect environment, His light and those allowed to release His light should have an impact on the ongoing process of creation. However, in the distant past, a cataclysmic rebellion affected this process. That rebellion enabled a dark force to dampen what we see as visible creation.

Scripture speaks of creation "crying out" for the sons of God to be revealed so things can be restored to their original order and balance. This restored order would be a far cry from the autonomic function around us that we have accepted as normal. In other words, everything is currently on autopilot, which dampens everything around us from expressing things that come directly from the Creator's heart as they were designed to do. We may miss much that was designed for us because we accept this "default mode" of darkness as normal.

In these last days, some are satisfied to have their relationship restored with the Creator as they accept His one and only Son, Jesus Christ, as Lord and Savior. There are, however, others who have been drawn deeper into the story of creation and are pressing in such a way that they have been challenged to use their "light" to answer the call of creation for a more complete restoration. To remove the dampening force so that creation can once again sing its song and reflect the way it was originally designed to be.

Many of us have discovered that a person cannot jump from step one in this process to step ten overnight. There are skill levels to be developed, and understanding needs to be acquired. We first work through the inversion of self to enable a more effective release of that inner light. Then, we can start impacting creation around us.

To be successful in this process, we have many resources to draw from, both spiritually and naturally. Because gemstones both send and receive frequencies and are greatly affected by intent and faith, they are a wonderful aid as we seek to address the fullness of scripture and restore what is around us. In essence, gemstones are frequency boosters that can help clarify things as we seek the face of God in the fulfillment of our earthly assignments.

Gemstones help us work past the static and filters of the soul and body as we seek clarity to grasp what our spirit has known all along. Because God is matter, spirit, and quantum, it is quite possible that the quantum link to His heart was lost in the fall. This would have tremendous ramifications.

I see that gemstones are like bicycle training wheels. They are simply physical tools that can help us clarify what our spirit already knows: the more often we engage Heaven, we will be able to see, know, feel, and hear what is being communicated to us. In this case, *familiarity breeds proficiency.*

Earth has its own operational platform with dampened frequency intensity. Heaven also has its own platform with much higher frequencies and the accompanying intentions of the Father's heart. Upgrading our ability to link powerfully with Father's heart is a game changer.

Let's look at how each medallion category can assist us. And don't forget how faith and intent are the energetic spark to power up what each medallion can do.

# Appendix C

## Flavia Diaz's Encounters

This is an encounter that Flavia Diaz had in June 2024. It exemplifies the importance of using anointed medallions to clarify our realms so that we see, hear, know, and feel with greater vision. It is also an example of a mature believer who regularly engages Heaven and the subsequent result.

This is the report Flavia forwarded to me after I sent her several medallions to try out. Be sure to visit my website at **Docrodich.com** for more information.

### Tuesday, June 25, 2024, 12:15 pm:

I opened the envelope containing the Immortality and Morning Star Medallion. As I handled the envelope, my head spun a bit, and I felt an immediate headache of about a 6 intensity. It might have been because I didn't realize I was wearing the glory medallion when I handled the envelope. When I opened the envelope, the headache went to about 7 in intensity.

I took off the glory medallion and stored it away. I placed the Morning Star and Immortality Medallions on my desk next to me and felt a very strong magnetic field around me. I felt a pull along with the headache and lightheadedness.

I stored away the Immortality Medallion in my closet. Then, I wore the Morning Star Medallion as instructed by the Holy Spirit. The Morning Star Medallion made me lightheaded and gave me a headache with an intensity of 5. My head also felt like it was inside a vacuum.

The headache waned away little by little in about 10-15 minutes, but a strange feeling of pressure lingered, especially on the top part of my head and my forehead. There was also a slight pressure around my eyes that lasted for about 10-15 minutes.

I kept the Morning Star Medallion on from 12:30 pm to 4:53 pm as I prayed, praised, and did other related work on my computer. The headache significantly lessened, but there was still slight pressure and lightheadedness. At 4:53 pm, I took the medallion off.

### 5:48 pm: Encounter with Jesus regarding "Why the Jump in Power"

I entered the help desk to inquire why such a jump in power when I handled the Immortality and Morning Star Medallions. The Lord Jesus came to me as I stepped into the help desk to inquire about this question. He took my hand, and off we went. We appeared in what looked like an astronomical observatory with a big opening, and we could touch the stars with our index fingers. When I looked at him, he was radiating rays of yellow light in which he got lost. I was also radiating that yellow light. That light then turned white, then green.

He said, "These are frequencies of my power and strength, causing the colors to change." I looked at a star twinkling in the distance, and its light transformed—first white, then yellow, green, purple, red, pink, and so on.

He explained, "It's all about the frequencies of my power."

He then asked, "Do you wish to shine and reverberate with the frequencies of my power so you can perform miracles and go where none have gone before? Connect and plug in with Me. Be intimate with me until we are one—Me in you, and you in Me."

He continued, "I am the Bright and Morning Star, and I show you how my brilliance can transform you. The medallions are a mere token of my brilliance and power. The closer your mortal body is to me, the stronger it becomes. Your spirit acts as a conduit for my power, reflecting it through your body. When your spirit is weak, it can't tolerate high levels of power, which drains the strength of your body."

**Answering my original question, he said:** "The energies[5] your body gives off contrast with the tune of the frequencies of the stones; therefore, they clash and cause discomfort to your physical body. When there's disease in your body, great levels of constructive energy can be debilitating to a weak compromised body. If the body isn't well, it will also affect your spirit, soul and vice versa. All three are supposed to work like a well-tuned orchestra. When you introduce high levels of energy and frequency, your body responds well if it's in good shape or whole, negatively if it's not. Your energy is low and faulty, so when confronted with this level of power at once, it was too much for your body."

---

[5] I got the understanding that he was very intentional in the words and prepositions he used.

Start by wearing the Morning Star Medallion only when you enter Heaven for a little while. As you build your spirit, soul and body, you'll tolerate it for longer periods. The stones each carry a specific property and energy that can be used for healing and restoring, it can also be used for destruction if used for malicious purposes.

### Wednesday, June 26, 10:30 am:

As I was getting ready to start the day earlier today, a thought from the Holy Spirit came to my mind to wear all cotton clothes. He has been telling me for a while to get rid of polyester and mixed-fabric clothes as much as possible and to wear natural fibers instead, so I wore all cotton[6] today, along with the Morning Star Medallion.

Unlike yesterday, I only felt a barely noticeable sensation (hard to describe) on the top of my head on both sides of my head. It was not uncomfortable, but I did feel some pressure there. I believe that the good frequencies of the cotton enhanced my own weak frequencies, allowing me to tolerate

---

[6] Synthetic materials are problematic when we are attempting to operate at higher frequency levels.

the medallion's frequency better. I think that yesterday, when I had the headache, it wasn't just my weak body's frequencies[7] but also the negative frequencies from the polyester clothes I was wearing that caused a shocking effect when I encountered the frequencies of the Morning Star Medallion.

Today, as I began the Declaration for the Soul and aligned my realms, I saw in my mind's eye a DNA strand being coated by a thin golden sheet that floated in, turning it golden as well when I reached the part 'release the DNA design of Jesus into my DNA.' As I continued reading and arrived at the section about the soul being liquid fire, connecting my spirit to my heart and body, and transferring that fire and heavenly things, I noticed new insights and questions arising. For instance, how can the soul transfer things to the spirit? How does this process work? I always thought it was the spirit transferring to the soul and the soul to the body. How can the body transfer things to the soul? How does this interplay work? I made a note to ask the Help Desk.

---

[7] Note: *See what the Lord Jesus told me on 6/25/24.

**Thursday. June 27, 2024, 10:45 am:**

I wore cotton again today, along with the Morning Star Medallion, and didn't experience any discomfort. I only felt a very faint energy from the top of my head towards my neck area. I began to worship and speak in tongues, and the pressure seemed to lessen. The longer I wore the medallion and spoke in tongues, the less I felt the effects on my head.

I wondered how the negative frequencies of my two computers and cell phone interacted with the medallion's frequencies. I had no way of measuring that.

As I continued, despite the interruptions at home, I heard the Holy Spirit say that I had an appointment at the Help Desk.

At the Help Desk, Jerry and Maria greeted me, and Jerry began to speak.

Jerry said, "The Morning Star Medallion you're wearing is a powerful specimen—a prime example of concentrated power. Do you think you can internalize and act upon that level of power[8] here on Earth, now?"

I replied, "If Heaven wills, anything is possible."

He said, "All things are possible with God. But there's a period of preparation. Just as your soul's bandwidth must expand, so too must your body and spirit. As it says in Revelation (Rev. 2:28), the Lord Jesus will give His own the Morning Star. Do you think that's only for the afterlife, or is it also for now?"

"I think it's for both now and later," I answered.

He nodded. "Correct. Do you know why the Lord is called the Morning Star?"

"No," I replied.

"It's because He is the 'first fruits' (1 Corinthians 15:20), shining the brightest among His brethren. That same glory is imparted to you. Just as the scientific community recognizes the Morning Star—Venus—as the first to appear in the early

---

[8] I understood that he was now speaking of Jesus' power, the ultimate Morning Star, which the Morning Star Medallion represents.

hours, the Messiah, the Firstborn, appeared to many in His splendor after the resurrection. Yes, He rose in glory in the early hours (Luke 24:1-16).

"The Lord gave Dr. Rodich a formula for a similar energy source, one that can clear environments of anything opposed to the brightness of His splendor. That's why you noticed new things yesterday when you read the script for your soul. His brilliance brings to light what was previously unseen, now made visible."

I asked, "What else does the medallion do?"

Maria replied, "It causes you to have a greater understanding of spiritual matters because it penetrates the deep parts of your spirit, not just your physical body. Your spirit is prepared to receive understanding and revelations from Heaven. It may be hard to believe that simple mineral stones can affect your spiritual being, not just your body. But remember that all three parts are attached, and now that you are aligned because you've done the alignment of your realms, they are more sensitive to one another. Each realm is more sensitive to one another and remember that your quantum realms are also affected by this energy.

"First in the physical, then in the spiritual (1 Cor. 15:46). The veil between the two is thin, and as a son, you have exercised your senses and can travel between the two with ease. This is why when you sense a bad environment or an evil spirit, your spirit picks it up, and your body's hair stands on edge. The same thing happens when you sense the presence of God; your body gets goosebumps, jerks, or falls under His weighty presence. In other words, what happens in one realm is felt in another.

"Tomorrow, try wearing the Immortality Medallion, and after a day or so, we'll talk more."

I thanked Jerry and Maria, and they replied, "You're welcome," before leaving.

### Friday, June 28, 2024, 9:37 am:

I wore cotton again today. After starting to praise the Lord, I put on the Immortality Medallion. I didn't feel anything physically. However, I wondered if this lack of negative reaction was related to the fact that I frequently saturate myself with what I call the 'No Death in My Body' or 'Immortality Scriptures.' I keep these verses at the back of my Aligning My Realms Script and declare them over myself once I've aligned my realms.

Today, my mom kept interrupting me by coming into my space where the sewing machine is to fix a couple of her clothes. This took all morning and a good part of the afternoon. I worked on another project I had to complete. By the evening, I was too tired to visit the Help Desk to inquire about the Immortality Medallion.

Yesterday, when Maria said, 'Let's meet in a day or so,' they knew I wouldn't be able to meet with them today.

FYI—These are the "No Death in my Body" or "Immortality Scriptures" I use:

1. Hebrews 2:14-15
2. 2 Timothy 1:10
3. Revelation 1:18
4. Romans 7:5-6
5. Romans 8:1-4
6. Romans 6:14
7. Romans 4:16-17
8. Romans 8:11
9. Psalm 92:12-14
10. Genesis 18-14
11. Psalms 103:5
12. Job 33:25-26
13. Isaiah 40:31
14. Jeremiah 30:17
15. I Peter 2:24

16. Psalm 107:20
17. Psalm 118:17
18. Job 10:12
19. 1 Corinthians 15:22
20. Joel 2:25-27

**Saturday, June 29, 2024, 8:15 am:**

Today, I wore the Immortality Medallion along with cotton clothing. As I stepped into the Help Desk today, Mark, an angel who works at the Help Desk and was assigned to answer my questions, greeted me. He said, "The Father has graciously allowed me to speak with you."

Mark continued, "You are correct; the scriptures are within your body. Remember, His Word is spirit and life (John 6:63) and is alive and active (Hebrews 4:12). The frequencies in those scriptures and the Immortality Medallion complement each other." As he spoke, I envisioned two wavelengths in harmony: one white and the other green,[9] with hints of blue flowing just beneath the white.

---

[9] I understood that it's green because it represents healing and life.

I asked, "What am I seeing?"

Mark explained, "You are witnessing the energy and power flow of God's Word established in you versus the energy of the stone in the Immortality Medallion.[10] The top white wavelength belongs to the Immortality Medallion.

"The green wavelength was established as a foundation in you. That's why it's towards the bottom."

He added, "Because the life wave of the scriptures that you've been declaring and sending to your body, soul, and spirit is close in agreement to the stone's energy and wavelength, it created, let's say an aura of positivity, beneficial to your mortal body and gave it strength and regeneration.

"Your faith in the scriptures plays a part. Since you believe in what you call immortality scriptures, this has empowered your body, soul and spirit to better absorb the constructive power of the Word of God and the similar energy of the stones in the Immortality Medallion. Instead of

---

[10] I understood that he referred to the 'energy flow of the stone' instead of talking about multiple stones because, in a way, all the stones combined produce a single energy flow. In other words, the energy from each stone becomes a unified flow of energy.

shocking your body, the energy and power of these two flowed in agreement and delighted your body. The Immortality Medallion's energy went straight through you without a contrary wave or energy obstruction."

I responded, "Wow, that's awesome."

Mark smiled and replied, "Yes, the Father and Lord Messiah love you very much. Keep up the good work, and visit us more often. We love you here and have so much more to share with you."

I thanked him, saying, "Please tell the Father, the Lord, and all of Heaven that I love them too."

Mark said, "Thank you. We'll talk again soon," and the encounter ended.

<u>Note:</u> *He was answering my question that came to my mind the previous day about the "No Death in my Body" or Immortality Scriptures.

### Saturday, June 29, 2024, 9:29 pm:

Reflecting on what the Lord Jesus told me about the Morning Star Medallion and what Mark shared about the Immortality Medallion, I sensed a potential contradiction. I returned to the Help Desk for clarity, and Mark came to assist.

He explained, "It's not a contradiction. There are areas in your body and soul that still need healing, which is why the energy and frequency emitted by the Morning Star Medallion caused those areas to respond negatively. Meanwhile, the Immortality Medallion's frequency and energy are more aligned with the immortality scriptures that your spirit, soul, and body are attuned to or saturated with. The more you immerse yourself in these immortality and healing scriptures and continue the work of healing and deliverance for yourself and future generations, the more healing and immortality your body will receive, enabling you to tolerate high frequencies of all sorts."

I responded, "So—the immortality scriptures circulating within me act like a shield, or rather a sponge, that absorbs the frequency from the Immortality Medallion."

Mark nodded, "You could put it that way. They both have similar frequencies (Immortality Medallion and Immortality Scriptures)."

I replied, "I understand now. Thank you."

Mark said, "You're welcome," and left.

### Sunday, June 30, 2024, 8:30 am:

I couldn't sleep last night, likely because I wore the Immortality Medallion all day yesterday without taking it off for a break. I felt extremely energetic throughout the day until I went to bed at midnight. As I mentioned before, I didn't feel anything specific while wearing the medallion, but it seemed to emit a very subtle yet powerful energy.

When I woke up this morning, after not having slept, I felt only slightly tired. This sentence is clear and conveys your intended meaning. I heard the Lord say to wear the Immortality Medallion only during the ecclesia service today. He also told me to rest and come up to him because he wanted to talk to me. I went up, and he began to speak to me about personal matters.

# Appendix D

## Medallions

**The Energy Daytime and PM Rest
& Contemplation Set**                  **$105.00**

This basic set is ideal for anyone looking to enhance dream clarity and reduce exposure to electromagnetic frequencies (EMFs). While the full impact of EMFs on our bodies and minds is still being researched, we know they can influence us on multiple levels. The Energy Medallion offers protection by blocking up to sixty-five percent of EMFs and includes carefully chosen gemstones to enhance subtle energies, helping you feel more balanced and focused during the day.

To support relaxation, the PM Medallion helps you unwind in the evening while also providing EMF protection.

*Note: Be sure to remove the Energy Medallion by early evening, as its energizing properties may otherwise interfere with your sleep.*

### The Sleep Medallion                                    $105.00

Designed to block up to 85% of EMFs during sleep, this medallion combines specially chosen gemstones that support rest and promote deeper, more restorative sleep.

### The Pain Medallion                                     $105.00

While this medallion was designed to ease those wandering aches and pains, it also does an excellent job of changing EMF patterns that cause migraine headaches.

### The Weight Assist Medallion                            $105.00

By converting personal energy and EMF signals into frequencies that enhance cellular function, this medallion supports weight loss when combined with a balanced diet and regular exercise.

## Engagement Medallions

**Quantum Emotional** $155.00

This medallion helps us work on our emotional base and how we process stress and past hurts. With it, we can tie into the Father's emotional realm and reformat our own into His image.

**Quantum Heart** $155.00

This medallion helps us connect directly with Father's heart. This is important because until we see ourselves as He sees us, we will not be able to function in the full scope of Sonship.

**Light/Essence/Arche** $155.00

This transformative three-part medallion facilitates a profound connection with both your inner light and the Father's light. It enhances engagement with creative essence, empowering you to interact with the creation around you in meaningful ways. Additionally, it allows you to reconnect with your original design from ages past, reinforcing confidence in the unique, wonderfully made nature of your being.

**Engaging Holy Fire** $155.00

Scripture reveals that God is Light, Love, and Fire—each expressing essential aspects of His nature. Other descriptions we encounter in Scripture help us understand His qualities more fully. Fire, in particular, acts as a profound cleanser. It has the power to purify us on many levels, removing impurities and strengthening what is good. We all need time in an environment where His refining fire can eliminate the dross within us, leaving only what is true and enduring.

**Engaging Glory** $155.00

We all benefit from a clear vision of God's honor and magnificence. Like all medallions, they serve to elevate our understanding and inspire us to embrace a higher standard of living. Through these symbols, we hope to receive and embody the qualities of His greatness in our own lives.

**The Seer Medallion** $155.00

Like its namesake, this medallion will help boost frequencies so we see better in our way of engaging Heaven. It may even boost a person's dream life.

### The Breath of Life Medallion $155.00

This medallion is for the more advanced Kingdom seeker where, rather than depending on Earth's physical oxygen as their source of life, that person relies on the Breath of God. While we are still learning exactly what this looks like, there is no doubt that pressing into higher realms for a higher design will serve us well in the future.

### The Ephod $155.00

These are the twelve stones worn by the Jewish High Priest (or gemstones with identical frequencies). This is a true governmental medallion focusing on getting answers on governing self, family, job, finances, and our geographical area. It has a lot of energy, so choose wisely when to use it.

### The Mazzaroth $205.00

This very high governmental medallion helps us govern from the cosmos, especially the part where our personal story is written. We are still learning the nuances of this medallion, so feedback is always welcome.

### The Morningstar $205.00

Like the Mazzaroth, this medallion denotes an even higher Cosmic calling in some ways. According to 2 Peter

1:19, we have an indication that when the greater release of Christ in us takes place (it's a process), there should be an exponential release of our light and His light in the areas of our focus. This is obviously worth looking into.

### Immortality                                                     $205.00

We are still learning about this; however, we know that immortality is promised in numerous scriptures, not just Heaven. How do we get there? This medallion will undoubtedly help.

I can say that this is so powerful that unless you have your scriptures ready and your focus in place, it may cause headaches or discomfort. It is obviously not for the faint of heart or to be worn as just jewelry.

### Engaging 3-D Reality                                      $205.00

While like the essence part of the Light/Essence/Arche medallion, this medallion is for engaging the fabric of 3-D reality to see what you have been called as a son or daughter to engage and bring to a higher design. This can be on Earth or the near cosmos as it relates to anything that creation is crying out for as long as it is part of God's design.

### The Destiny Medallion                                $255.00

This medallion is what Heaven says; it is the gemstone that will best help you fulfill your scroll and engage your destiny. It takes a voice print to draw from and then many hours of testing the hundreds of gemstones available to choose from to assemble your special medallion. You could say this is the frequency equivalent to the nutritional workups I do.

### Doc's Face & Wrinkle Cream                          $30.00/jar

This blend of healing and essential oils rejuvenates your skin and helps remove the smaller wrinkles while lessening the bigger ones. Many ladies also use this as a base for their makeup.

The cost is $30 per jar, and unless accompanied by a medallion order, they are shipped in sets of two.

# Description

*What if the mysteries of quantum physics could unlock a deeper understanding of God's Kingdom?*

In *Unlocking the Quantum Kingdom*, Dr. Robert Rodich takes readers on an enlightening journey to explore how the latest scientific discoveries intersect with ancient spiritual truths. Grounded in a background of ministry and holistic healing, Dr. Rodich delves into quantum physics to illuminate how we, as believers, are uniquely designed to demonstrate God's power and purpose here on Earth.

This book reveals that the answers to humanity's deepest questions have always been within reach. Our limited understanding has veiled these truths, but through "expanded thinking" and a renewed intimacy with God, we can begin to access the Kingdom in transformative ways.

**Inside *Unlocking the Quantum Kingdom,* discover:**

- **The Intersection of Faith and Quantum Science** – How recent discoveries in quantum mechanics mirror principles of God's creation and reveal His boundless design.
- **Unlocking Spiritual Technologies** – Insights into spiritual tools hinted at in Scripture, often overlooked but essential for fulfilling our divine assignment.
- **A Call to Deeper Intimacy** – The importance of cultivating a personal relationship with God to experience His presence and understand our role in His plan.
- **The Groanings of Creation** – How quantum principles can guide us to respond to creation's call for restoration and wholeness.

Step into *Unlocking the Quantum Kingdom* and embrace a vision of God's Kingdom that's vibrant, dynamic, and closer than ever before.

## About the Author

Dr. Robert Rodich, author of *Unlocking the Quantum Kingdom* and *Moving Toward Sonship*, is a dedicated scholar of the quantum realm and its profound connections to spiritual growth. With a long-term fascination for how quantum principles can inform and deepen one's understanding of faith, Dr. Rodich's writings invite readers into a journey of exploration that challenges the boundaries of traditional spirituality. This book offers practical insights into how quantum ideas can transform perspectives and lead to personal empowerment and spiritual awakening.

Dr. Rodich shares his life with his wife, Laura, and together, they are blessed with a large family of seven sons and eleven grandchildren. His family has been a continual source of inspiration, encouraging him to explore how science and spirituality intersect to unlock potential within us and our world. Dr. Rodich's work inspires those seeking a deeper connection to the divine through the fascinating lens of the quantum kingdom.

For inquiries, contact him at:
**Email:** doc.rodich@gmail.com
**Website:** docrodich.com

Published by:

A division of LifeSpring Publishing

www.scrollpublishers.com

Has God spoken to you about writing a book?
Let us help you!

www.ingramcontent.com/pod-product-compliance
Lightning Source LLC
Chambersburg PA
CBHW020907090426
42736CB00008B/531